RUTLAND

CW00419803

Photographs by RICHARD ADAMS

Gazetteer by GILLIAN DICKINSON

BARROWDEN BOOKS
RUTLAND

Published by Barrowden Books,
15 St Mary's Grove, London N1 2NT
Distributed by
Barrowden Books, c/o Rutland District Council,
Catmos Street, Oakham, Rutland

All rights reserved, No part of this publication may
be reproduced, stored in a retrieval system, or
transmitted in any form or by any means, electronic,
mechanical, photocopying, recording or otherwise,
without the prior permission of the copyright
owners.

Photographs copyright © Richard Adams 1984
Text copyright © Barrowden Books 1984

ISBN 0 9508989 1 0

Printed and Bound in Great Britain by
Smith Settle, Otley, W. Yorkshire

Acknowledgements
We would like to acknowledge the financial
assistance of Rutland District Council and Anglian
Water Oundle Division in the publication of this
booklet. We are also grateful to Leicester County
Council for the provision of information and to
Bryan Matthews for reading the text of the
Gazetteer though the publishers take
responsibility for any mistakes. Photographs on
page 11 and 13 are published courtesy of Anglian
Water Oundle Division and those of Rutland
Museum, Edith Weston Turret Clock and the
interior of Oakham Castle, courtesy Leicester
County Council.
Photographs on the title and contents pages are of
Lax Hill and the Welland Valley, with Tixover
church in the background

CONTENTS

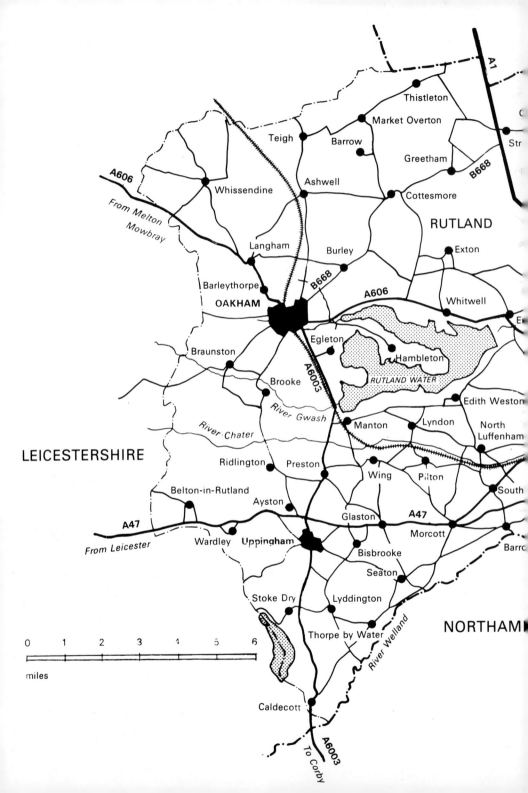

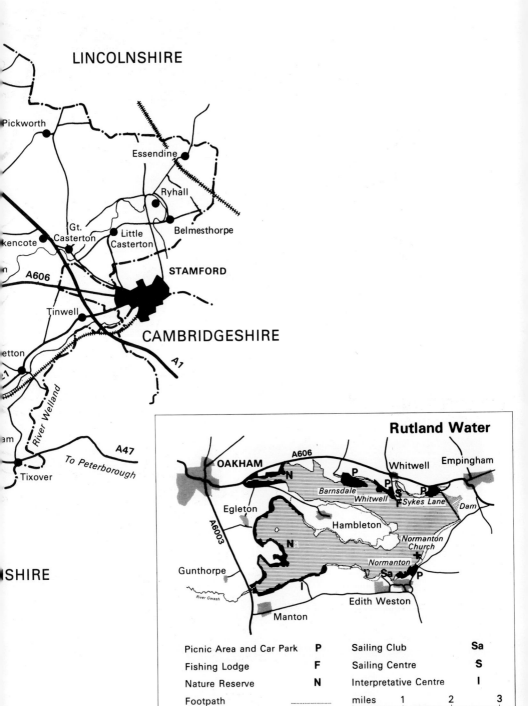

LINCOLNSHIRE

Pickworth

Essendine

Ryhall

Gt. Casterton

Little Casterton

Belmesthorpe

kencote

A606

STAMFORD

Tinwell

CAMBRIDGESHIRE

etton

A1

River Welland

am

A47

To Peterborough

Tixover

SHIRE

Rutland Water

OAKHAM

A606

Whitwell

Empingham

N

Barnsdale

P

P

Whitwell

S

P

Sykes Lane

Egleton

F

Dam

A6003

Hambleton

N

Normanton Church

Gunthorpe

Normanton

N

Sa

P

River Gwash

Edith Weston

Manton

Picnic Area and Car Park	**P**	Sailing Club	**Sa**
Fishing Lodge	**F**	Sailing Centre	**S**
Nature Reserve	**N**	Interpretative Centre	**I**
Footpath	....	miles	1 2 3

Old stables of Martinsthorpe Hall

INTRODUCTION

Ten years ago Rutland ceased to be England's smallest county and became a district of Leicestershire. Two years later, during one of the driest summers on record, the new Rutland Water started to fill, gradually drowning some of the best land of a predominantly agricultural county. 'The anomalous little shire', the words used by the 1958 Boundary Commission, had become the home of the largest man-made reservoir in Europe.

The reorganization could have been worse: the Commission had proposed dismembering the county, merging Ketton rural district with Lincolnshire and putting the rest of Rutland into a new county to be created out of Huntingdonshire, the Soke of Peterborough, the Isle of Ely and Cambridgeshire. Rutland County produced a powerful 'Case for Rutland' and circulated a petition against the proposal in thirty-seven parishes. An average of eighty per cent of the electors in each parish voted against it and in five villages it was a hundred per cent; surely a record for a democracy anywhere in the world.

Rutland won in 1960 and there were great celebrations, with the brewing by Ruddle's Brewery of a special Victory Ale. The crunch came in 1974; as the result of another reorganization, Rutland ceased to exist as a county. Yet Rutland, as an identity, most emphatically survived. Ratepayers address their letters to Rutland District Council, the Rutland County Museum continues with an active programme of special exhibitions and lectures about Rutland's history, and there is a new Rutland Record Society. Rutlanders remain very proud of their distinctive buildings and their two great public schools at Oakham and Uppingham which this year celebrate their quatercentenaries. And now there is Rutland Water, which has brought great changes and many new visitors.

Many of these visitors will come, first, to see the reservoir, to sail, sailboard or fish. Others will be bird lovers and will appreciate the great increase in numbers that such a dramatic change in the habitat has brought about. Before 1976 only about two hundred acres or one five-hundredth of the surface of Rutland was water. Apart from four small rivers – the Welland, with its tributary the Eye Brook, the Gwash, and the Chater – the only water was the artificial ponds at Burley-on-the-Hill and Exton. There were no attractions for the water- and marsh-loving birds. Today Rutland Water offers a surface area of 3,100 acres and a 350-acre nature reserve which provides a sanctuary for a great variety of wildfowl and hides for ornithologists. The Reserve is now internationally important for wintering wildfowl and is recognized as the most important inland site in Britain for wading birds on migration.

This guide is also for those who want to see our many attractive stone villages, and to discover what Rutland has to offer the walker, the cyclist, the curious searcher after lost villages, the architectural historian or church buff. For these visitors the gazetteer offers a first taste of what you can find. Those who want more information could not do better than visit the Brian Kennedy room in the excellent library at Oakham, which is also a tourist information centre.

THE LAND Rutland, like everywhere else, owes its buildings, its agriculture and some of its entertainments (particularly hunting) to its underlying geology. The rivers rise in the west, the highest part of the county. This is clay, with outcrops of sandstone and marlstone, and was heavily forested through most of the middle ages. A large area of this forest became the King's Royal Forest of Leighfield in the thirteenth century and remained under forest laws until the early 1600s. The cleared forest later became excellent pasture land, for the heavy boulder clay was hard to work with the plough, and by the end of the seventeenth century hunting the fox over open ground began to replace the traditional deer hunt in the forest. Organized fox-hunting began in 1730 when five great landlords each subscribed three hundred pounds to a United Hunt. A few years later the county was divided between two hunts which subsequently became the Belvoir and the Cottesmore.

To the north of the county a rather bleak and windswept plateau extends from Burley to Thistleton with, at its centre, Cottesmore Airfield. The eastern part of the county is Rutland's share of the oolitic ridge that runs from Dorset through the Cotswolds to the Yorkshire coast. It is more broken country and through its centre the River Gwash meanders to join the Welland river east of Stamford. It is here that the best building stone, the Lincolnshire limestone in its many colours and varieties, is found. It has been quarried since the early middle ages at Ketton, Edith Weston, Casterton, Clipsham and at Barnack and Ancaster outside Rutland. Collyweston, just over the county boundary in Northamptonshire, provided limestone slabs for roofing. Because of this superb, very hard-wearing stone, Rutland has some of the finest medieval churches in the country.

Rutland's southern boundary is formed by the River Welland; across the valley are fine views of Northamptonshire villages on rising ground to the south.

HISTORY Historically, Rutland *is* rather curious. It never became a Midland shire as did other parts of the old Kingdom of Mercia in the tenth and eleventh centuries.

Nor did it take its name from its most important town, like Leicestershire, Lincolnshire, Northamptonshire or Nottinghamshire. The name 'Roteland', which probably refers to the redness of the ironstone, is used at the beginning of the eleventh century to mean an area smaller than the present Rutland whose capital may have been Hambleton. This territory was bequeathed by Edward the Confessor to his wife, Edith, who gave her name to Edith Weston. At the time of the Domesday Survey (1086) it was divided, one half being accountable for taxation to Nottingham, the rest of it a part of Northamptonshire. Rutland is first called a county, the Norman name for shire, in the reign of King John. Until the sixteenth century most of the land belonged to the King or the Church. After the Dissolution of the Monasteries, and increasingly in the seventeenth century, the great families, the Digbys of Stoke Dry, the Noels of Exton, the Finches of Burley, the Heathcotes of Normanton, and the Cecils of Burghley, just outside the county, gradually accumulated more and more land. This process was accelerated by the enclosure acts. The ownership of land led to political power and through most of the nineteenth century Rutland was represented in Parliament only by Noels, Finches or Heathcotes.

RUTLAND TODAY The past wealth of Rutland is reflected in the architectural quality of the market towns of Oakham and Uppingham and of many of the fifty-one villages which contain twenty-five conservation areas and over seven hundred listed buildings. However, many of the villages suffered from the housing boom in the 1960s and early 1970s, and efforts are now being made to confine new housing to Oakham, Uppingham and a few of the larger villages.

In spite of the post-war decline in agricultural employment and the extractive industry the population of Rutland rose from 20,000 in 1951 to 32,000 in 1981. This was largely because people employed in the nearby large towns found Rutland an attractive place to live in. New cement, textile and plastics industries; the establishment of two prisons, two air bases and the expansion of the schools of Oakham and Uppingham did not provide sufficient employment within Rutland and efforts are now being made to encourage more industry to come to the area. With the construction of Rutland Water the district is learning to adapt to its new role as a tourist centre. Good road connections to the remainder of the country and to Leicester, Peterborough and Nottingham, are encouraging the development of leisure activities which complement the rural character of the district.

RUTLAND WATER

In the 1960s it was predicted that the current supplies of water could only satisfy the rising demand for water from Northampton, Peterborough, Corby, Milton Keynes, Daventry and Wellingborough until the 1970s. The scheme to create a storage lake of 27,300 million gallons by damming the valley of the River Gwash above Empingham, and drawing also on the Welland and the Nene rivers, was agreed after sixty-four alternative options had been rejected. Parliamentary approval was given to the project in May 1970, in spite of opposition, primarily from the National Farmer's Union and the County Council. The Welland and Nene River Authority set to work and in 1974 it handed over the project to the Anglian Water Authority.

The dam is constructed mainly from Upper Lias Clay obtained from the land which was subsequently flooded. The crest is 1,200 metres long and forty metres above the lowest section of the base, which is 810 metres in cross-section. The maximum depth is thirty-four metres. The water is treated and processed at the treatment works at Wing. A network of pipes provides water to thousands of customers in Northamptonshire, Leicestershire, Peterborough and Milton Keynes.

Today Rutland Water, managed by Anglian Water's Oundle Division and sympathetically landscaped, is rapidly establishing itself as a water sports and leisure centre of national importance.

Sailing and Sailboarding Rutland Water is the training ground of the Olympic Sailing Team, and its irregular shape and huge area of two thousand acres of sailing water make it attractive to sailors of all standards. There is usually a good breeze out on the open water for the expert sailor, while the Hambleton and Whitwell peninsulas provide more sheltered conditions for the less experienced.

The Day Sailing Centre, at Whitwell Creek, is open every weekend and Bank Holiday from 1 April to 30 October. There are changing rooms, showers and toilets. Dinghies and sailboards may be launched here for a small fee and craft can be hired. An experienced sailing master will supervise launchings and inspect craft for safety. He also advises on weather conditions and if there is racing in the vicinity which should be avoided.

The Rutland Water Rescue Service, staffed by well-trained volunteers, is on call at weekends and Bank Holidays during the season to help all water sports enthusiasts.

The Rutland Sailing Club, Edith Weston, has a well-appointed clubhouse and mooring. Membership is open and the club has around a thousand craft, making it one of the biggest inland clubs in the United Kingdom. Approximately a hundred different types of sailing craft are based at the reservoir, and races are held for Contender, Enterprise, Fireball, 505, Flying Fifteen, Kestrel, Mirror, Optimist, Wayfarer, catamaran, cruiser and sailboard. There are also courses of Olympic standard.

The Rutland Sailing Club Residental Centre has been developed for schools, clubs and other organizations. There is accommodation in dormitory style with excellent catering facilities, changing rooms and showers. All enquiries should be directed to the Secretary, Rutland Sailing Club, Gibbett Lane, Edith Weston. Telephone Stamford 720292.

Sailing on Rutland Water

A satisfied fisherman

Fishing Rutland Water is one of the finest still-water fisheries in Europe, stocked with both brown and rainbow trout reared in Anglian Water's own trout hatchery. About fifty thousand anglers fish at Rutland Water each season. Most seasons produce well over sixty thousand trout weighing more than fifty tonnes – an average of two pounds per fish. Rainbow trout approaching ten pounds and browns of over twelve pounds have been landed. One angler hooked eight fish weighing a total of forty-eight pounds, a record for a European reservoir.

National and international club competitions and events are held at the fishery which has a fleet of sixty powered boats, a spacious lodge, a well-stocked tackle shop, a fish-gutting room with freezer, and a comfortable lounge for prize presentations. Whether you are a newcomer or a seasoned visitor to Rutland, Anglian Water's wardens will always make you welcome and will be pleased to give you information on tactics. Telephone Empingham 770 (during season, April to October).

Eye Brook Reservoir This reservoir is just off the A6003 Uppingham/Corby road. There is fishing for rainbow and brown trout from the bank or from boats which are available for hire. The Reservoir is listed by the Nature Conservancy as a Site of Scientific Interest and is a bird sanctuary. The only facilities are a fishing hut, with an attendant on duty and boats to hire. Telephone Rockingham 770264.

Cycling Rutland Water Cycle Hire Centre, Whitwell, near Oakham, hires cycles for all age groups, including an adult tricycle with two children's seats. Children under sixteen must be accompanied by an adult. The traffic-free tracks round Rutland Water are especially suitable for cycles. You can also cycle along the highway to nearby villages. Telephone Empingham 705/Stamford 720513.

Walking There are footpaths through the woods and along the shore of Rutland Water, and around Hambleton Peninsula. The Nature Trail extends approximately one mile between Whitwell and Barnsdale picnic sites.

Picnic Sites There are beautifully landscaped picnic sites beside Rutland Water at Barnsdale, Whitwell, Sykes Lane and Normanton car parks. All have toilet facilities and permanent kiosks which provide refreshment. Sykes Lane also has an adventure playground.

For further information on Rutland Water, contact the Reservoir Manager, Frank Knights, the Old Hall, Whitwell, Oakham. Telephone Empingham 321.

Wildlife Since the construction of Rutland Water the wildlife has returned to the area surrounding the reservoir. Rabbits, hares, foxes, badgers and even the occasional fallow deer can be seen. The reservoir is also a natural sanctuary for thousands of wild birds. Records show that more than 218 species have been seen since the project began.

Winter. The winter wildfowl population builds to a peak in December and January with almost every species sighted in full breeding plumage. Mallard, teal and shoveler stay close to the shoreline while the diving ducks – pochard, tufted and golden-eye – stay further out. Smew, scaup and goosander can also be seen. On the banks are flocks of wigeon and coots, and small groups of greylag geese. Mute swans are year-round residents, but winter also brings occasional Bewick's swans from Siberia. They can be identified by their yellow and black bills.

Summer and Autumn. More than seventy-two species of breeding birds have been recorded, from the great-crested grebe to the woodpecker and kestrel. Autumn brings dunlin, green- and redshank to the exposed shorelines of the reservoir. Huge flocks of swallows, martins and swifts feed on insects.

Woodland In the four years before the reservoir reached its maximum level, oak, ash, · beech and wild cherry trees and shrubs of hazel, field maple, spindle and dogwood were planted. An enclosed area has been set aside at the entrance to Barnsdale car park to show the various trees used in the landscaping of the reservoir. This arboretum is open to the public for most of the year and is well worth a visit.

Nature Reserve At the western end of the reservoir the Nature Reserve, managed by the Leicestershire and Rutland Trust

Disabled people in a hide

for Nature Conservation, covers 350 acres which stretch nine miles along the perimeter of the Water. The southern shoreline is open to the public and includes an area of natural woodland and several specially-created habitats for local wildlife. A Visitor Centre for the Lyndon Section will be completed during 1984 with an information centre to cater both for the casual visitor and for organized parties. The section of the Reserve with access at Egleton is also open to the public. Eleven hides overlook the Water and at Egleton there is a specially adapted hide for wheelchair bound visitors.

Along the northern shoreline is an area restricted to researchers. For further information about the Trust contact The Warden, Fishpond Cottage, Stamford Road, Oakham, Rutland, Leics. Telephone Oakham 4101.

Archaeology During excavations for the building of the dam some interesting archaeological sites were discovered. Before 1965 the only visible archaeological evidence in Empingham was the medieval moated site close to the centre of the village. However, some time before the Rutland Water project was announced, a farmer unearthed a bronze Anglo-Saxon brooch. Such finds are usually made when excavating cemeteries as it was customary to dress and equip the dead for their journey to the next world. A limited excavation revealed a cemetery of fourteen inhumations.

Archaeologists working in the area also discovered two Romano-British agricultural sites, both recognized from material – pottery, bone and stone – ploughed to the surface of the fields. Further excavation revealed farm outbuildings. The largest structure was an aisled barn used for light industrial activity and perhaps for housing farm workers. Outside there was a well and

Skeleton from Saxon grave

13

other smaller structures, one of which is occupied by a corn-drier. A large area of the site was cobbled with ironstone and limestone blocks to form a yard.

Excavations on these sites lasted three seasons (1969–71); the contractors then arrived to start earth-moving activities. But the archeological discoveries caught the imagination of the construction team and four more important sites were uncovered and partially excavated. Earth-scrapers cleared at least two Anglo-Saxon *Grubenhäuser* (small wooden huts with a timber floor set over a hollow) and a gully, dug mostly for drainage purposes, which surrounded an Iron Age hut. In June 1974 scrapers clearing an area for Sykes Lane car park found several skeletons which led to the excavation of a larger cemetery (135 graves) of Anglo-Saxon date. The graves were of men, women and children and many contained distinctive grave goods. Male burials were often accompanied by a spear, shield or knife. Female burials were decorated with brooches, beads, bone combs and other trinkets. Children had few metal goods in their graves though there was often a pot. No grave cut into another, so we must imagine a system of grave marking that has left no trace.

The western edge of the cemetery followed the line of an earlier Iron Age trackway which, although silted up at this time, must still have been visible. A section has been left as a sunken hollow leading from the car park to the water's edge.

The latest discovery was made in the summer of 1976 when it was realized that an area being cleared for a car park about half a mile south of Whitwell contained substantial traces of Iron Age and Romano-British occupation, extending over about five acres. The evidence of wooden and stone structures, pottery and metalwork suggests a series of buildings associated with people following an agricultural life.

Other Things to See and Do

Up-to-date information on opening times and prices of admission are included in the Supplement.

Museums

RUTLAND COUNTY MUSEUM, Catmos Street, Oakham. Telephone Oakham 3654. The Museum occupies a converted eighteenth-century Riding School. It exhibits local crafts and craft tools, agricultural implements and wagons, and stages special exhibitions.

RUTLAND RAILWAY MUSEUM, Cottesmore Road, Ashwell. Telephone Leicester 676376. A working exhibition of steam trains and railway stock.

STAMFORD MUSEUM, Broad Street, Stamford. Telephone Stamford 55611. Exhibits objects of local historical importance.

STAMFORD BREWERY MUSEUM, Scotgate, Stamford. Telephone Stamford 52186. Housed in a nineteenth-century brewery, with copper vats, a steam engine and a shire horse.

MELTON CARNEGIE MUSEUM, Melton Mowbray. Telephone Melton 69946. Illustrates the past and present life of the area and has displays of Stilton Cheese and Melton Pork Pies.

NORMANTON TOWER, Normanton. Telephone Empingham 321. Situated on the edge of Rutland Water and reached by a causeway. The Tower will open in 1984 as a Water Museum.

Historic Buildings (further details of Rutland buildings are contained in the Gazetteer).

OAKHAM CASTLE, Telephone Oakham 3654. A Norman Banqueting Hall which survives from a twelfth-century manor

Rutland County Museum

house. It contains a unique selection of horseshoes presented by Royalty and peers of the realm when they passed through the manor of Oakham.

BEDE HOUSE, Lyddington. Telephone Uppingham 2438. A fine fifteenth-century range of buildings originally built as a palace for the bishops of Lincoln.

TOLETHORPE HALL, Little Casterton. Telephone Stamford 54381/56133. A sixteenth-century manor house with eighteenth-century additions. It is the headquarters of the Stamford Shakespeare Company who perform in the open air theatre in the grounds during the summer months.

BURGHLEY HOUSE, near Stamford. Telephone Stamford 52451. An outstanding example of late Elizabethan architecture, with famous painted ceilings, a large art collection, tapestries, china and a medieval kitchen. The surrounding deer park was landscaped by Capability Brown.

Normanton Tower at night

PRIEST'S HOUSE, Easton-on-the-Hill. Telephone Stamford 2616. A pre-Reformation priest's lodge of architectural interest, with a small museum of village bygones.

KIRBY HALL, Deene, near Corby. Telephone Corby 3230. A sixteenth-century house with seventeenth-century alterations by Inigo Jones. It was abandoned in the late eighteenth century.

DEENE PARK near Corby. Telephone Bulwick 361/223/278. Deene was acquired by Sir Robert Brudenell in 1514 and has been lived in since by his descendants, including the 7th Earl of Cardigan who led the Charge of the Light Brigade. There is a park and extensive gardens, with a large lake.

ROCKINGHAM CASTLE, near Corby. Telephone Rockingham 770240. This is now a mainly Elizabethan House within the walls of a Norman Castle. There are fine collections of pictures and china. The house has extensive gardens containing a tilting lawn and a sixteenth-century yew hedge.

GRIMSTHORPE CASTLE, near Bourne. Telephone Edenham 222. A large quadrangular house converted from a medieval castle. There is a good collection of eighteenth-century portraits and furniture.

Archaeological Sites

WING MAZE. A circular turf maze forty feet in diameter, perhaps associated with religious penance.

BURROUGH HILL. An Iron Age hill fort with some excavations exposed, between Twyford and Somerby. Its high location and a toposcope give the visitor extensive views over East Leicestershire. A pamphlet, 'Leicestershire Burrough Hill Iron Age Hill Fort', documents the fort's history and is available from the Department of Planning and Transportation, County Hall, Glenfield, Leicester. Telephone Leicester 871313.

Cattle at Farm Park

Farm and Country Parks

RUTLAND FARM PARK, Uppingham Road, Oakham. Telephone Oakham 56789. A working farm with rare breeds of cattle, sheep and ponies. The park and woodland have facilities for picnicking, and there is a shop.

EAST CARLTON PARK. Telephone Rockingham 771296. Parkland with nature trails, information centre, rural crafts and a steel-making heritage centre.

Picnic Sites, Trails and Walks

WAKERLEY WOODS. Extensive Forestry Commission woodland with nature trails and picnic areas.

YEW TREE AVENUE, Clipsham. Forestry Commission picnic area close to the magnificent yew-tree avenue that was once the main entrance to Clipsham Hall.

THE VIKING WAY. This long-distance walk stretches ninety miles from the Humber Bridge to Oakham. Further details from the Department of Planning and Transportation, County Hall, Glenfield, Leicester. Telephone Leicester 871313.

Yew topiary at Clipsham Hall

Towns and Villages of particular interest

The towns of Oakham and Uppingham and the villages of Empingham, Exton, Ketton, Lyddington and Market Overton are particularly worth visiting. For further details see Gazetteer.

STAMFORD Described by Sir Walter Scott as 'the finest scene between London and Edinburgh' the old town of Stamford remains largely unspoiled with many beautiful seventeenth- and eighteenth-century houses and several great medieval churches. Stamford has five hundred 'listed' buildings and is designated an outstanding conservation area.

Markets

General markets are held in Oakham Market Place on Wednesdays and Saturdays and in Uppingham Market Square on Fridays. There is a cattle market off South Street, Oakham, on Fridays.

Theatres

Uppingham Theatre, Stockerston Road, Uppingham. Telephone Uppingham 3955/3318.

Stamford from the meadows

Rutland Theatre. Telephone Stamford 54386/56133. The Stamford Shakespeare Company has a summer season of outdoor productions at Tolethorpe Hall, Little Casterton, near Stamford.

Shows

RUTLAND WATERSHOW. A two-day show with water events and exhibition stands, held over the May Day Holiday weekend.

BURLEY-ON-THE-HILL SHOW. An annual charitable event which includes show jumping, local competitions and stands. It is held on the Spring Bank Holiday.

RUTLAND AGRICULTURAL SHOW. Held in the grounds of Burley-on-the-Hill. A two-day traditional agricultural show with classes for stock, show jumping, driving etc. It also has stands and other events. It is held on the first weekend in August.

BURGHLEY HORSE TRIALS. An international three-day event is held early in September.

Sports

Swimming

The swimming pools listed below are open to the public on a limited basis; for details telephone the appropriate number.

Vale of Catmose Pool, Oakham. Indoor pool. Telephone Oakham 2286.

RAF North Luffenham Pool. Limited public use. Telephone Stamford 720041 ext. 319.

Ransborough Hall Leisure Centre, Langham, near Oakham. Outdoor pool. Summer use for Club members. Club membership easily purchased. Telephone Oakham 2984.

Tennis

Oakham Tennis Club, The Vale, Oakham. One court for public use. Telephone Oakham 2042.

Bowls

Oakham Bowls Club, Lime Kiln, Oakham. Non-members welcome. Telephone Oakham 3621.

Squash

Ransborough Hall Leisure Centre, Langham. Two courts available for public hire. Telephone Oakham 2984.

Vale of Catmose Community Sports Hall. For hire to the public at weekends and during school vacations for badminton, table tennis etc. Telephone Oakham 2577.

Golf

Luffenham Heath – eighteen holes. Telephone Stamford 720205.

Stoke Rochford Golf Club – eighteen holes. Telephone Great Ponton 275.

Burghley Park Golf Club, Stamford – eighteen holes. Telephone Stamford 62100.

Melton – nine holes. Waltham Road, Thorpe Arnold. Telephone Melton 62118.

Riding

Bradley Lane Stables, Clipsham, near Oakham. Telephone Castle Bytham 335. Tuition and escorted hacks.

Manor Farm Stables, Hambleton. Escorted rides around Rutland Water. Telephone Oakham 2160.

Manton Lodge Stables, Manton, near Oakham. ABRS approved; BHSUU tuition; escorted hacks. Telephone Manton 269.

Stretton Riding and Driving Centre, Manor Bungalow Farm, Stretton, near Oakham. BHS approved, qualified instruction in riding and driving; private or class tuition. Hacking out if required. Telephone Castle Bytham 323.

Fishing

Rutland Water and Eye Brook. (See Rutland Water and Supplement).

Information

Further information on local facilities is available from

Rutland District Council. Telephone Oakham 2577.

The Tourist Information Centre, Oakham Library. Telephone Oakham 2918.

The Citizens' Advice Bureau, High Street, Oakham. Telephone Oakham 3012.

Information Centre, Rutland Water, Whitwell. Telephone Empingham 321.

Anglian Water Oundle Division publishes a series of free leaflets about Rutland Water which can be obtained at the Centre.

GAZETTEER

Ashwell lies in the Catmose valley at the junction of the main road north from Oakham with the road from Whissendine to Cottesmore. If you come from Oakham you pass the famous Cottesmore hunt kennels and, opposite, Ashwell Open Prison. The old wishing well, which has a modern well-head with moral inscription, is at a bend in the road, just as you come into the village.

The village is in a rough square, with a stream running through the middle down Waterlane – a street with some good seventeenth-century houses. The manor is known to have been held by King Harold before the Conquest but by the time of the Domesday Survey (1086) it had passed to the Tuchet family who lived here until 1515. A fourteenth-century hollow oak effigy of an armoured knight in the south chapel of the church probably commemorates one of the family. There is also an early sixteenth-century alabaster effigy of a priest, almost life size, with some remains of original paint.

In 1851 St Mary's was expensively and dramatically restored by the distinguished architect William Butterfield, who also built the appealing lych gate. Note particularly the chancel roof decorated in bright colours in the typical Butterfield style. The architect was also commissioned by the patron, Viscount Downe, to build five almshouses. They surrounded a yard to the north of the church which became known as Widows' Yard and is now the Post Office and village shop.

The village had at least two rectors whose names have gone down in history. At the time of the Civil War Thomas Mason, an ardent Royalist, was expelled from his living and left for Belvoir Castle to command a company in the King's name. More recently, the Reverend James William Adams became the first clergyman to win a Victoria Cross by a spectacular act of bravery during the Afghan War (December 1879). His memorial is a rather undistinguished grave just south of the church door.

On the road to Cottesmore you cross the old Melton Mowbray-Oakham canal. It had a short life for not long after it was finished it was bought out by the owners of the new Midland Railway Company and closed.

Ayston is definitely a squire's village, dominated by the early nineteenth-century Hall whose kitchen garden seems to have encroached on the green. A fire in 1830 destroyed many cottages and others have been pulled down since; now there is little building earlier than the nineteenth century. But the modern building, like the old, is in ironstone and in keeping with the few early houses in the village. It is all very pleasant, although noisier than it used to be for the roundabout for the Uppingham bypass is just south of the village. The Old Rectory, to the north of the Hall, was rather inconsiderately pulled down in 1858 by Sir Henry Fludyer, fourth baronet, when he was Rector and had no use for it. His successor lived in a farmhouse east of the green which was extended by pulling down three cottages – the sundial from one of them is now above the church porch.

The house passed from the Fludyer to the Finch family in 1873 when the heir to the last baronet, Katharine Fludyer, married a Finch. But Sir Arthur Fludyer lived in the Hall until his death in 1922 and it was only then that the Finches moved in. The church, which lies just south of the lawns of Ayston Hall, is mostly thirteenth- and fourteenth-century. The restoration of 1897 left the old box pews and an elegant eighteenth-century font. There is

Hounds at Cottesmore Hunt Kennels, Ashwell

Entrance to Ayston village, with park on left

Warning to vagrants at Barrow

some fifteenth-century glass, with almost complete figures in the east window of the south aisle, and some interesting glass – mostly sixteenth and seventeenth century – found at the Hall about 1900.

A much-defaced effigy, probably of a knight and his lady, lies just outside the south porch of the church. It does not depict 'two industrious one-armed twins' as one guide has claimed.

Barrow, a small village south of Market Overton, takes its name from the hill on which is stands. The remains of earthworks north-east of the green must have vanished when the modern houses were built. The village has an old market cross and this was probably the centre of the old village which may once have been larger than Cottesmore to which it was ecclesiastically attached. There are some remains of the old chapel-at-ease, which ceased to be used in the late seventeenth century, in the garden of the Church House (not on view). Its last Rector scandalized visitors by not wearing a surplice and allowing his congregation to keep their hats on and remain seated throughout the services. The chapel was replaced in 1831 by a small Gothic Revival church which was finally pulled

down in 1974 after it had become very dilapidated.

To the west the land falls away and there are fine views. There is a pleasant walk down the hill west of the green on a sideroad which joins up with the main road to Teigh.

Barrowden lies on the southern border of Rutland. If you come from the south (Wakerley), you cross the River Welland over a fine fourteenth-century bridge, later widened, with a carved face on one of the arches. Fossils, washed out of the marl-

Wakerley bridge across Welland

St Peter's, Barrowden, from village

Looking across pond to Exeter Arms, Barrowden

stone, can often be found in the river pools.

Barrowden was probably settled very early and became an important centre in the fourteenth century, with a weekly market and an annual fair. In 1550 the Manor was granted, by the terms of Henry VIII's will, to Princess Elizabeth 'until she make a suitable marriage'. A year later the King's Councillor, Sir William Cecil, later Baron of Burghley, became the owner and until early this century the Cecils owned most of the village. Barrowden Heath was enclosed by the Exeter Estate in 1882 – the last enclosure in Rutland – but twenty

Tombstone in cottage wall, Barrowden

acres were made into allotments and several acres were kept for a recreation field, now the green. The old pound is still there.

The church, at the extreme west end of the village, has a beautiful fourteenth-century spire and is remarkable for the width of the nave and aisles in relation to their length. It was extensively repaired in 1876 when for some reason the seventeenth-century pupit was given to Harringworth church just across the river; Barrowden kept only three panels which were made into a reading desk. Near the church are several interesting houses and cottages; the

most notable is Durant Farmhouse which faces east across the green and pond. The church has a fine Renaissance monument to Rowland Durant (1588). The Victorian school, closed just before two new housing estates were finished, is now a private house; Carey's House (eighteenth century) is named after the Rector who built it. Almost opposite the Rectory, an old tombstone with a chiselled inscription has been built into the wall of a cottage. Chapel Lane, to the east of the green, is named after an attractive Baptist chapel (1819).

A pleasant walk past the old mill leads across the meadows to Wakerley from where there is a striking view of the church with Morcott windmill on the horizon. It is worth visiting the redundant church at Wakerley for its unusual capitals with scenes of knights besieging a city. Past the church are Wakerley Woods which are full of bluebells in the spring and picnickers in the summer.

Belton – since March 1982, Belton-in-Rutland – was a settlement in the Forest of Leighfield which covered the hills of West Rutland and a small portion of East Leicestershire. It is a delightfully individual village on the side of a steep hill, about half a mile north of the modern A47. The Eye Brook forms the southern boundary. A glance at a large-scale map shows how the settlement grew from a horseshoe space, surrounded by houses which were connected by a track. Later, another road developed to link the ends of the back gardens, and the west side of this is still known as Backside Lane. In the thirteenth century the church was badly damaged by fire and in 1776 there was another fire in which twenty-seven houses were completely burned. However, the village still has many charming houses of the seventeenth and eighteenth centuries, most of them of ironstone. Littleworth, which is said to have had some cottages saved from the fire, now has entirely modern housing.

The church (St Peter) has a beautiful thirteenth-century font and an alabaster slab in the chancel floor with incised effigies of some sixteenth-century Haselwoods, owners of the Old Hall. There is also a monster's head (perhaps carved by the creators of the gargoyles) which forms a drain in the south aisle.

The Old Hall, next to the church, dates from the early seventeenth century. Further west is Westbourne House, a two-storey ironstone eighteenth - century house, banded with limestone. In front of the church is the War Memorial which has built into it the King's Stone, where Charles I is said to have rested after his flight from the Battle of Naseby, though he couldn't possibly have done so as he fled in the opposite direction!

Bisbrooke ('Bitel's Brook') straddles an ironstone ridge between two valleys on the borders of Northamptonshire. To the south ran the railway; to the north one can hear the busy A47. Until 1918 the village was part of the Belvoir estate owned by the Duke of Rutland, and it used to be famous for its market gardens. The Misses Stokes in 1953 (*Just Rutland*) commented that 'almost everyone grows and sells strawberries'. Today the gardens have been replaced by a lot of modern housing, both in brick and stone, though some good ironstone cottages and farmhouses, dating from the sixteenth to the eighteenth centuries, remain. The Gate Inn, perched above the southern valley, is probably named after the kissing gate which leads to a bridle path to Uppingham. There is also a right-of-way over the Inhams, originally a piece of manorial ground. The present church was built in 1871, replacing a small thirteenth-century building with a traditional Rutland double bellcote. The

first vicarage disappeared in 1575 and was probably the reason why the unfortunate Vicar, Simon Palmer, and his wife, El╷n, 'did lay in the church from Christmas until Candlemas Day last and abused that place too shamefully to be writed'. Bisbrooke Hall is, rather surprisingly, about half a mile north of the village, on the other side of the A47.

Braunston is near the Leicestershire border and within the bounds of the old royal forest of Leighfield. To the north Flitteris Park was enclosed as a hunting

Pagan figure, Braunston

park by Richard, Earl of Gloucester, son of King John and Lord of the Manor of Oakham, in 1250. It now survives only in the name of a farm. Around the village are the remains of several earthworks, and an old sunken road, the Old Leicester Lane, crosses the parish. Chiseldyne Farm is reputed to date from 1604 and is named after the family that held the manor during the fourteenth and fifteenth centuries. The brass of Kenelm Chiseldyne (1597) is in the church. Chapter Farm, south of the church, is largely Elizabethan. Quaintree Hall, previously Cedar House, has a

Seventeenth-century house, Braunston

Georgian front but encloses a medieval hall and may be partly built from stones taken from Brooke Priory when it was pulled down in the sixteenth century. A building attached to the house – perhaps an old tithe barn – has a thirteenth century window in the gable.

The church is largely fifteenth century, with earlier remains, and has been much restored – especially in the nineteenth century. Outside the west door is a roughly carved stone, perhaps a fertility symbol. For many years it had lain face down and was used as a doorstep. To the west of the churchyard runs a footpath, known as the Wisp. This was originally a piece of land and is first mentioned in a document of 1299. In 1584 it contained fourteen acres of wood and pasture.

Opposite the church there is an attractive stone and brick bridge across the River Gwash which has its source near the village.

Brooke, wrote the historian W. G. Hoskins, is 'one of those remote little places (though only two miles from Oakham) which one instantly feels is a personal dis-

Brooke in snow, from south

covery to be treasured and visited again and again'. Like Braunston, the parish was formerly within the forest and originally belonged to the manor of Oakham. From the middle of the twelfth century it was owned by the Priory of St Mary's. In 1549 it came into the Noel family who became Earls of Gainsborough in 1682, and the parish belonged to the Gainsboroughs until 1925 when the estate was broken up. Most of the village has now disappeared.

Nothing now remains above ground of the original priory though the grass banks in the fields probably cover monastic foundations. The Noels built Brooke House on the site but all this sixteenth-century building has gone too, except for a ruined gateway and an octagonal porter's lodge which became a dovecote in the eighteenth century. The present charming red-brick house, known as Brooke Priory, dates from the seventeenth century and incorporates some remains of the monastery. There used to be a large pond in the Town Park opposite, formed by an ancient dam, and this was proably part of an early settlement.

The church (St Peter's) is enchanting

Burley House from the south

and lovingly cared for. Part of it is Norman (tower, south doorway, north arcade and font) but the chancel, chapel, north aisle and south porch were rebuilt by the Noels in 1579, an unusual time for church building. It was entirely refitted and all the furniture dates from the late sixteenth or early seventeenth centuries. In the chancel are two high, square-backed pews, with seventeenth-century graffiti. In the north wall of the chancel there is a beautiful canopied alabaster monument to Charles Noel (d. 1619). Nearby are gravestones recording the death of Henry Raullins and his five wives: the last outlived him.

The Old Rectory, opposite the church and now a farmhouse, is said to be the oldest house in the village. It has a leper's hole.

Burley-on-the-Hill is now known mostly for the great Palladian house, built by Daniel Finch, second earl of Nottingham, between 1694 and 1708. This was probably the third house on the site. In 1603 Sir John Harington of Exton entertained James I in his Burley House when he was on his way south to receive the crown.

George Villiers, the powerful Duke of Buckingham, built the second house which was described by the diarist John Evelyn as 'among the noblest seats in England'. It was at a banquet here for Charles I and his Queen, Henrietta Maria, that Jeffrey Hudson, the dwarf – then a child of only nine inches high – was served up in a cold pie. The house was besieged and burnt by the Parliamentary forces though the stables remained. In the last half of the eighteenth century the terrace to the south was built by Repton whose 'Red Book' is kept at the house. In 1815, the present house narrowly

1920s, became famous for being used on Cherry Blossom boot polish advertisements in the 1920s. The Finches Arms, now Chesnut Farm, closed in the early nineteenth century.

The church, which is connected to the house by a passage, was handsomely restored by J. L. Pearson in 1869–70. It has a fine marble monument by Chantrey to Lady Charlotte Finch, who was governess to the children of George II and Queen Charlotte. The church has lately been made redundant but can still be visited.

North-east of the village, near Alstoe

Old smithy at Burley

escaped being purchased and demolished by the Duke of Wellington who wanted to build a new palace on the site. Instead, a grateful nation gave him the estate of Stratfield Saye in Hampshire.

In 1908 there was a serious fire while Winston Churchill was staying in the house. Part of the interior was destroyed. The great avenue leading south from the house was cut in half by the creation of Rutland Water and the house now looks over the reservoir.

Only a few houses in the village remain. The smithy on the green, in use until the

House, is a motte-and-earth castle of the twelfth century. The name commemorates the meeting-place of the hundred of Alstoe in the tenth century.

Caldecott is an attractive ironstone village on the southern borders of Rutland at the junction of the Eye Brook and the road north to Uppingham. There may have been a Roman settlement here; Roman tiles are said to have been found when the church was restored in 1862–3. There is a lot of new building though several sixteenth- to eighteenth-century houses re-

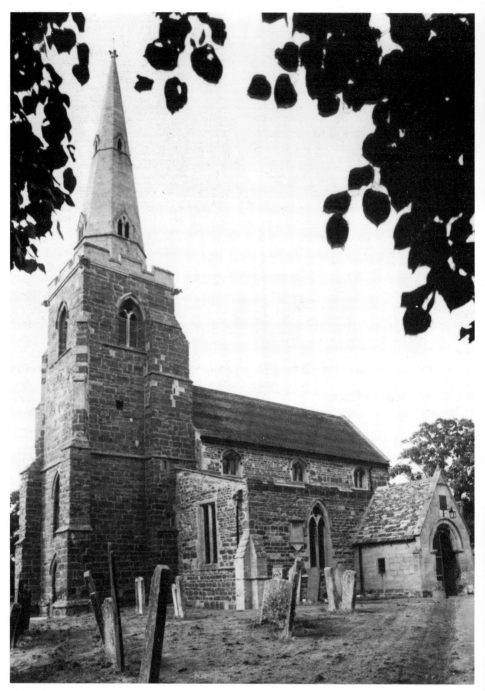

St John's, Caldecott

main – some with date stones and often with alternating bands of limestone and ironstone. Two pubs survive: the Plough, which replaced the Old Plough (1578–1948) – opposite and now a private house – and the Castle. There were two crosses, one at the top of the village where three roads meet and the other on the Green. Some of the stones are said to have been built into the wall of the Black Horse pub which used to stand to the north of the green on the site of the present village hall. At one time Caldecott used to be a refuge for deerstealers who operated in nearby Rockingham Forest.

In 1797 the spire of the church was 'shattered by lightning' and in the 1950s the broken tip was still kept in the church porch. St John's was much restored in the nineteenth century when the rare sanctus turret was replaced on the new nave. It was removed, after being damaged, in 1976. It is said that in 1780 the Rector removed a number of gravestones to pave his kitchen in Gretton. The church has recently been handsomely repaired, thanks to a very generous local bequest.

The Eye Brook used to flood regularly, the most recent floods being in 1884 and 1922. The building of the Eye Brook reservoir in 1940 largely removed the threat of flooding.

Clipsham lies to the north of the county along the road from the A1 to Stretton, on the borders of Lincolnshire. Most of the houses are built from the oolitic limestone from the famous quarries near the village which were worked from the thirteenth century until the 1950s. One of the most recent uses of the stone was to rebuild the House of Commons after it was bombed in 1941. In 1556 a mason, writing to Sir William Cecil about the stone he should use at Burghley, remarked that the 'best stone for stairs is to be had at Clipsham.'

Seventeenth-century farmhouse, Clipsham

The stone was also used for roofs.

Clipsham Hall, an attractive two-storey, eighteenth-century house, was also built of the local stone. It stands with the church in a park, north of the village. East of the house, and once the main drive, is a topiary of yew trees, created in the 1880s by the Head Forester, Amos Alexander. The topiary is cared for by the Forestry Commission and is open to the public. Some of the trees seem to have lost their original animal shapes but this is a very pleasant place for walks, with a car park and picnic area.

In the village two attractive seventeenth-century farmhouses face each other.

Cottesmore has given its name to a famous hunt whose hounds were bought from Mr Thomas Noel by Sir William Lowther and moved to Cottesmore in 1740. There have been several archaeological finds in the area, notably the Bronze Age Cottesmore Hoard (discovered in 1906) which can be seen in Rutland Museum. The church, St Nicholas, has a seventeenth-century pulpit on a modern base and a strange font whose bowl is a thirteenth-century capital, used upside down, which is said to have once been a mounting block at Cottesmore Hall. Peter Gunning, the author of the prayer 'for all sorts and conditions of men', was rector here for nine years in the seventeenth century.

The Hall was seriously damaged by fire in 1926; it was repaired and used as a hunting box but was pulled down in 1974 to make way for a new housing estate. Cottesmore House, where the Noels had lived until the 1930s, was struck by lightning and burned to the ground in the 1950s.

In 1935 Cottesmore airfield was built. It was an American base from 1943–5 and now houses the Tornado aircraft.

Three-nation crew, with Tornado, Cottesmore

Turret clock, Edith Weston church

Edith Weston belonged for a time to Edith, wife of Edward the Confessor and daughter of Earl Godwin. It was probably the most western of her Rutland possessions – hence the name. The attractive limestone village, originally built round a green, now stands on the southern edge of Rutland Water, with the sailing club to the west.

The church, St Mary's, looks a bit strange from the outside because in 1865 the Rector built another chapel on the south side, completely changing its appearance. Inside, there is a very beautiful late Norman north arcade and other features of interest – notably the Heathcote memorials, some of them brought from St Matthew's, Normanton. There is also a simple memorial, erected by the Anglian Water Authority, to those who had been buried in the churchyard of Normanton. Their remains were removed and cremated before Rutland Water was built. A rare Commonwealth Turret Clock (1658) belonging to the church is now in Rutland Museum.

West of the church, facing north across Rectory Lane, is the Old Rectory, a distinguished gabled building of 1627. The present rectory is a farmhouse. Nothing now remains of the Old Hall, which abutted the church on the north side, and houses have been built on land previously occupied by the old stables. The later Hall (1830, by Vulliamy) has also gone; it was burned, repaired and finally demolished in 1957.

Egleton belonged to the Finches of Burley who sold part of the estate in 1926 but retained all the land they could see from the house until 1948. The present road to Burley was built when the common fields were enclosed, the villagers being allowed to pasture one cow and five sheep. One suspects that some cottages north of the church proved eyesores and were removed – there are tell-tale mounds in the fields.

The church is very interesting with a well-preserved tympanum over the south door – it is now thought to be Saxon. A part of the old rood screen is under the tower arch and there are the remains of a Royal Arms above the chancel arch. In the chancel are some interesting eighteenth-century framed slate memorials.

The old Manor House is now the Home Farm. It has an attractive dovecote, unfortunately joined to a modern brick building. At the east end of Main Street is the entrance to one of Rutland Water's Nature Reserves, for Egleton now stands on the shores of the reservoir. You leave your car in the car park and walk.

Empingham now stands above the dam which created Rutland Water and at one time there was a plan to call the reservoir after this ancient market town. The suffix 'ingham' suggests a very early Saxon settlement and recent excavations uncovered some Roman buildings south of the village. Empingham was a prosperous place during much of the middle ages, with a substantial population and a three-day fair. To the west of the village are traces of a moat, all that remains of the Normanvilles' Manor House.

In 1470, during the Lincolnshire Rising, there was an important battle north of the village when a local force, led by Sir Robert Welles, was routed by the Yorkist forces led by King Edward IV. After the battle – also known as the Battle of Losecoat Field because the fugitives threw off their distinguishing coats to escape unnoticed – Warwick the Kingmaker, who was suspected of instigating the rising, was forced to flee to France, finding support from King Louis XI.

The Earl of Ancaster owned most of the village until 1924 and, when Normanton Park was enlarged in the eighteenth century, Normanton village was swept away and the villagers moved to Empingham. The estate offices were housed in the Prebendal House, a fine eighteenth-century house beside the church.

The church is large and striking, with a tall and impressive fourteenth-century tower and spire, with very high pinnacles. Until about 1870 it was under the direct jurisdiction of the bishops of Lincoln. Because there was one very conservative vicar for most of the nineteenth century this beautiful church escaped a drastic restoration, keeping its singing gallery and

Chancel arch and Royal Arms, Egleton

St Peter's, Empingham, from south

painted pews until 1894. Inside, the church is largely thirteenth century, though there were many changes in the fifteenth century.

There are several new housing estates to the east of the village and many of the old thatched cottages have gone.

Essendine had an important Norman castle, given by Queen Elizabeth I to William Cecil who built Burghley House. From him it passed to his second son and one of the titles of the Marquis of Salisbury is still Baron of Essendine. The moat, north-east of the church and now over-grown, was still full of water at the beginning of this century and used to be a popular skating rink.

The most striking feature of the little church, which was probably the castle's chapel, is the twelfth-century south door-way with a tympanum showing Christ, flanked on either side by an angel. The sculpture on the outside of the doorway is now badly worn away and the church, though beautifully cared for, has very few parishioners. It was restored twice in the nineteenth century; a buttress against the middle of the west wall was taken down and the chancel rebuilt. Note the low-side window which remains from the earlier

Norman arch, St Mary's Essendine

building in the nineteenth-century chancel.

The main London to Edinburgh railway runs through Essendine and it was just north of the village, on Stoke Bank, that the famous steam locomotive, the Mallard, made the record of 126 mph on 3 July 1938. The substantial and attractive railway hotel is now a pub.

Exton, meaning 'ox-farm', is mentioned as early as 1185 as Exton Park – a wooded farm enclosed for huting deer. Exton was Rutland's largest park and once covered 1,500 acres. There is a great deal to see

Flying Scotsman passing through Essendine

here, both in the church and in the village. The manor belonged to the Haringtons, then from the seventeenth century to the Noel family, now the Earls of Gainsborough. The village was probably moved when the Old Hall was built and the parish church now stands on its own, south of the village, approached down a long lane. It has a most unusual spire on an octagonal base, surrounded by pinnacles in the shape of turrets.

To the north east of the church is a very good view of the ruins of the Old Hall which was burned to the ground in 1810. Elizabeth of Bohemia, the daughter of James I who became known as the Winter Queen, once lived here with her guardian, Lord Harington. The New Hall was built round an old farmhouse in 1850, in the Jacobean style, with a Roman Catholic chapel attached for the family. About the same time the church was largely rebuilt

Grindling Gibbons monument, Exton

Fort Henry, near Exton

by J. L. Pearson, an important Victorian church architect.

Anyone at all interested in sculpture will want to visit the church for its nine magnificent monuments, most of them commemorating Haringtons or Noels. The earliest, a tomb chest, is fourteenth century; there is also an outstanding Elizabethan wall monument attributed to Nicholas Johnson, and monuments by Grinling Gibbons (1686) and Nollekens (1766). High on the walls are Noel and Harington banners and funerary helmets. North-west of the church, in the park and on the edge of a lake, is a picturesque dovecote.

The village has many thatched cottages, some of them round an attractive village green with trees, and an excellent pub. Pudding Bag Lane has, rather unimaginatively, been renamed West End Lane.

Two miles north east of the church is Fort Henry, a pretty Gothick summer house, built on a lake in the eighteenth-century style.

Glaston is two miles east of Uppingham, most of the village lying to the north of the A47. The name comes from the Old Norse and an Saxon cemetery was found here in 1946. The church dates from the twelfth century and has an unusual and very short broach spire. The east window is nineteenth century and replaced a rounded window, shown in an 1830s drawing, which was probably put in to light a singing gallery. The Rectory, just south of the church, is nineteenth-century brick, surrounding an earlier stone house. There is an early eighteenth-century house west of Monckton Arms, still with mullioned windows, and a slightly earlier house to the east of the village. The old pond in Spring Lane has had its ramp, used to 'swell' the wooden wheels of carts to fit their iron rims, restored. The Old Hall (seventeenth century) and Glaston Hall, built from its materials, have now both been demolished. The long tunnel of the Manton-Kettering branch railway runs from the Glaston Road, south of Wing, to a point just south of the A47, passing Glaston to the east.

Great Casterton, also known as Bridge Casterton, takes its name from a Roman fort to the north of the village. The 'Bridge' carries the old Great North Road (to the west of the Roman road) over the River Gwash; the village has been by-passed by the modern A1.

The Roman fort to the north of the village was abandoned when a town, whose building started in the second century, was given defences. These can be seen very clearly from the Ryhall road. This large site – about eighteen acres, partly enclosed by the river – was investigated in the 1950s. A fourth-century villa has also been discovered to the north-east of the town. Nothing remains today of the villa but there are finds from all the sites in the Rutland Museum.

The church (St Peter and St Paul) was built in the south-west corner of the Roman town and is a lovely, unrestored thirteenth-century building. Note the early clerestory, with circular windows and the tall, round-headed arcades. The eighteenth-century pulpit still has its sounding board though the paint has recently been stripped off. In a recess in the south aisle is an effigy of a priest; there is another on the outside with only the head and feet showing (compare Hambleton).

John Clare (1793–1864), the poet who was born at Helpston in Northamptonshire, worked here as a gardener.

Little Casterton has an interesting small church which lies to the south of this limestone village, on the banks of the River Gwash. It was substantially restored in the nineteenth century by the Rector, Richard

Roman earthworks at Great Casterton

Tolethorpe Hall, Little Casterton

Twopeny, who is said to have rebuilt the chancel twice, having discovered – after his first rebuilding – that the thirteenth-century chancel had been shortened at some time. Inside, there are several things worth seeing: some good, late-thirteenth century painting around the west window; a piscina in the shape of a flower, said to have been brought from the ruined church at Pickworth; a Norman tympanum which was found at a restoration in 1908; and a very fine brass to Thomas Burton (d. 1381), owner of the Manor of Tolethorpe.

Tolethorpe Hall, whose medieval gatehouse survives, is the home of the Tolethorpe Shakespeare Company who perform outside during the summer. It was once the home of the Browne family, one of whose members, the Puritan Robert Browne, founded the Brownist sect, the forerunner of the Congregationalists. Unfortunately, this sixteenth-century building has been virtually gutted inside and its early eighteenth-century staircase has been removed.

Greetham, meaning a village on stony ground, lies just to the west of Ermine Street, that part of the Great North Road that runs from London to Lincoln. It is shaped like an E, with arms stretching north from the main road and connected by footpaths. William Halliday, a well-known Rutland stonemason who was responsible for repairing several of Rutland's churches in the nineteenth century, worked here. He was a bit of a magpie and an odd collection of stained glass, tracery and carvings found its way to his workshop in Great Lane. One of the churches he worked on was Exton where 'it is known that much good stonework was removed without apparent reason' (*Little Guide*). However much one may disapprove – and some of the Perpendicular tracery is in remarkably good condition – this strange building is fascinating.

Stonemason's house, Greetham

In 1860 St Mary's church was reported to be in a 'ruinous condition' with one of the bells 'half way out of the belfry window'. It was largely rebuilt in the late nineteenth century. In the west wall of the south aisle are some old stone fragments, including part of a Norman tympanum which must have survived from the twelfth-century church. The slender spire was 'blown out of the Perpendicular' in the late nineteenth-century and had eight feet rebuilt. Church Lane was formerly known as Sheepdyke Lane.

Edward I stayed at the Old Manor House, north-west of the church, whose site has now been built over. There used to be ironstone workings near the village and lime kilns which seem to have been worked intermittently from Roman times until the late nineteenth century.

Hambleton has lost much and gained much with the coming of Rutland Water. The three hamlets – Upper, Middle and Nether Hambleton – have become one village, marooned on a lozenge-shaped peninsula which is connected by a narrow neck of land to the Oakham road. To the north is a dramatic view of Burley House; to the south the hundreds of brightly-

End of the road, Hambleton

There was a church in Hambleton before the Conquest and the dedication to St Andrew could be a misreading of the Saxon name of St Audrey (or Ethelreda). The stumpy broach spire that you see when you enter the village belongs to a largely twelfth- and thirteenth-century building, expensively and well restored in the nineteenth century. There is an interesting Norman doorway.

Just south of the church is the Priest's House of the late sixteenth century, much restored. At the bottom of the hill is the Old Hall, on its own small peninsula. It is all that now remains of Middle Hambleton. Built in 1610, the Hall was sold to Abel Barker (who later moved to Lyndon) including 'all doors, wainscotts, locks, keys, glass, tables, forms, bedsteads, shelfs, thralls, utensils, etc'.

Back at the top of the hill is one of the best small hotels and restaurants in the country – Hambleton Hall. Noel Coward wrote *Hay Fever* in this Victorian house when it belonged to Mrs Astley-Cooper, one of the Bright Young Things. From the garden there are magnificent views south over the reservoir.

Ketton is named after the River Chater

coloured sails of the sailing club. It is a wonderful place for a summer's day but the quiet road that led along the hill-top to Normanton and the charming views across the valley of the Gwash are gone for ever.

It is probable that Hambleton was for a time the capital of the Anglo-Saxon kings in Rutland and the Hambletons remained important throughout the middle ages, with a weekly market and annual fair. A seventeenth-century house in the village is probably built on the site of the old manor of the Umfravilles and Badlesmeres who owned the village for many centuries.

Old Hall, Hambleton

which runs through the village, separating Ketton from the hamlets of Geeston and Aldgate. It probably derives from a Celtic word meaning 'forest stream'. The village has been famous since the early middle ages for its honey-coloured limestone. It is soft when quarried but hardens when exposed to the air and has been used for many cathedrals and churches, particularly in Norfolk and Suffolk. Many of the Cambridge colleges, the Law Courts in Fleet Street, the Earl of Nottingham's mansion at Burley-on-the-Hill, and the wonderful figures sculpture at Beverley Minster in Yorkshire, are also in Ketton stone.

The parish church, on one side of the long main street, is 'one of the finest in the East Midlands, lofty and dignified, with a tower and spire of superlative beauty' (Hoskins). There is also a very impressive Norman west front. Strangely enough, the church seems to have been built of Barnack, not Ketton, stone though Ketton stone was used for the many interesting headstones of the eighteenth century – see, especially, the one to a local mason. There is also a seventeenth-century gravestone, built into a wall to the east of the church.

In 1932 the Bishop of Lincoln granted an Indulgence to those who would help to finish the church, either with their labour or by giving money. It was restored by Sir Gilbert Scott in 1861–2 and was one of his best church restorations. The chancel was later remodelled by Sir T. G. Jackson, another distinguished architect who had been one of Scott's pupils. The present east window and altar, and the war memorial, are by Sir Ninian Comper.

There are many good limestone cottages in the lanes of Ketton. Opposite the church is the Priory with a sixteenth-century window and a Georgian porch. There is a pleasant walk down Mill Lane, past the old mill and to the west of the Priory, to the Barrowden road.

Norman west doorway, St Mary's, Ketton

Ketton Portland Cement Company, which started in 1928, is one of Rutland's only large industries. It employs about six hundred people.

Langham, a long, scattered village north of Oakham, is the home of Ruddle's beer whose fame has now spread all over the country. The brewery (to the south of the village) was started in 1885 by Richard Westbrook Baker, the steward of Sir Gerard Noel who owned most of the houses. Baker was an enterprising fellow who also invented a special Rutland plough. Langham has also given the country an Archbishop, Simon de Langham (1366–8). His alabaster effigy is the earliest in Westminster Abbey. The village is also said to have had a witch, Joan Flower, who was in service at Belvoir Castle where she was accused of procuring the death of the heir to the Earl of Rutland.

St Peter's was originally a chapelry of Oakham, and Whissendine, Langham and Oakham all have rather similar plans. The church is best seen from the south (the churchyard side) from where you get a good view of the great fifteenth-century window in the south transept. There is an unusual clerestory which continues round

Weathervane at Old Hall, Langham

Seventeenth-century arch, North Luffenham

the east wall of the nave with windows above the chancel arch. A small tributary of the Gwash, called the Dyke, runs along the west wall of the church and through the village. The best remaining cottages are in Church Street.

The Old Hall, next to the church, was built in 1665, with a west wing of 1926. Over the entrance is a charming little weathervane, with a clock on the house side and a compass on the other. At the end of the nineteenth century the owner of the Hall was Lieutenant Colonel Jervoise, a great benefactor of the church, whose grave is outside the south door.

Ranksborough Hall, just outside the village to the north, is said to be the site of an Iron Age settlement. It now has a caravan park, and squash courts.

North Luffenham was one of the earliest villages in Rutland to be settled. A Saxon cemetery (sixth to seventh centuries) has been found to the north of the village, and to the south is a medieval moat. The Hall, which was bought by Viscount Campden in 1636, was besieged by the Parliamentary forces under Lord Grey and was surrendered on conditions that were not kept. The church and house were pillaged and several houses were burnt down. The Hall, which had become very dilapidated, was finally pulled down in 1806 and Digby Manor House (just to the east of the church) then became known as North Luffenham Hall. This house was probably built by John Harington in the sixteenth century (his son built the large tithe barn beside the house) but was added to in the early 1900s. The old road, still a public footpath, ran south-west of the church to join up with the North Luffenham road. A pretty, seventeenth-century arch leads from Digby Drive to the garden of the Hall.

The Street and church, South Luffenham

The church, though rather heavily restored in the nineteenth century, is very well worth visiting. The fourteenth-century windows in the chancel, all with different tracery, are beautiful and have a lot of contemporary glass. There is an Elizabethan pulpit and several monuments to the Digbys, and a seventeenth-century plaque to Archdeacon Robert Johnson (1540–1625) who was 'observant, preached painfully and kept good hospitality'. He was also exceedingly charitable and founded both Oakham and Uppingham schools in 1584, as well as almshouses at Oakham and Uppingham.

South Luffenham is an interesting village to walk round for in 1850 the village became the first railway junction in Rutland and this created a new village south of the River Chater, with new roads. The old part is round the church whose tall, crocketed spire is a good landmark. The church dates from the twelfth century and is worth seeing for its powerful north arcade with two very wide Norman arches. It has the oldest dated bell in the district (1588) but this had to be recast in the middle of the nineteenth century when there were extensive restorations and the church gained a new and rather ugly round pulpit by G. E. Street.

Near the church is a seventeenth-century farmhouse and an old tithe barn, now a private house. To the south of the church is South Luffenham Hall, a handsome seventeenth-century house, rather like Lyndon Hall. The main street (called, simply, The Street) runs across the village to join up with Back Lane and two old rights-of-way, one leading west, past an old earthwork, to Pilton; the other south to Morcott.

The common lands lay east and south of the village and were bisected by a new station road, linking the Peterborough and Stamford Road. On the east part, south of Foster's Bridge, Lord Ancaster (who had owned the land since the enclosure) built a golf course.

Lyddington is two miles south of Uppingham, and the attractive ironstone houses, many of them with date-stones of the seventeenth and eighteenth centuries, stretch along the Gretton Road. It has a village green, just north of the Bede House, and its thirteenth-century market cross, which had been removed in the nineteenth century, was re-erected in 1930.

The main reason for visting Lyddington is the Bede House, for many centuries a palace of the Bishops of Lincoln who received the Manor of Lyddington from William I at the Conquest. The house, with its high chimneys and buttresses, now dates from the fifteenth century when much of it was rebuilt. It was seized by Henry VIII in 1547, and in 1551 Edward VI gave the manor to Lord Gregory Cromwell, the son of Thomas Cromwell. Shortly afterwards it was granted to Sir William Cecil of Burghley. In 1602 his son, the second Lord Burghley, converted the building into an almshouse and the name 'Bede' dates from this time because those who lived there were expected to pray ('biddan') for their benefactors. There is a very fine hall, with a beautiful wooden ceiling of the first half of the sixteenth century, and the rooms of the bedesmen and women can be seen on the ground floor. The Ministry of Works began to repair the building in 1945 and took over twenty years to finish the admittedly very handsome restoration.

The church, with its Perpendicular arcades and their very tall piers, was largely rebuilt in the fifteenth century, perhaps at the same time as the Bede House. At the east end are the Communion rails of 1635 which enclose the altar on all sides. This

Bede House, Lyddington, from south

was supposed to be a tactful compromise between the views of Archbishop Laud, who required the altar to be against the east wall, and the Puritans who wanted it in the body of the church. Note the blocked-up door in the north aisle by which the bishop would enter the church from his palace, and the 'acoustic' jars high up in the chancel, put there to improve the sound. There is a brass to Edward Watson (d. 1520) of Rockingham Castle with an inscription in the new Roman lettering.

To the south of the church is the 1626 Priest's House which has lost most of its mullions, and to the west is part of the old wall which enclosed the palace. At the corner is an octagonal turret with a public footpath through it. To the east of the church can be seen remains of the bishops' fish ponds.

Lyndon is a pretty, secluded village with a small green, a church, some pleasant stone cottages and two Halls. Lyndon Hall, probably built by John Sturgis between 1671 and 1673, is to the west of the village; Top Hall, in a similar style and about the same date, is appropriately sited on the top of a hill to the north. Gilbert White, the naturalist of Selborne, stayed at Lyndon Hall often and mentioned Lyndon in the *Natural History*. His sister was married to Thomas Barker of Lyndon (1722–1809), one of the first meteorologists. He also wrote an account of Lyndon for the first reprint of Wright's history of the county. There are gravestones of the Barker family against the churchyard wall.

The church has a rather strange Norman font, with crude serpentine carvings. It was found in the churchyard during the extensive 1866 restoration when the church was given a grand and unattractive pulpit and reredos, both in alabaster.

45

Lyndon church, with stable block of Hall

If you follow the Lyndon road to the main road you come to the Lyndon Nature Reserve at the other side of the crossroads.

Manton is at the western end of Rutland Water. To its east is the Lyndon Nature Reserve; to its west a public footpath leads across the Oakham road to the old stables of Martinsthorpe Hall – all that remains of Martinsthorpe, whose village disappeared before the Hall was built in 1622. Manton has an extraordinary church, especially from the west where it is dominated by a huge thirteenth-century bellcote, built of ironstone. The chancel, however, was completely rebuilt in the eighteenth century and has large Georgian windows which make the church very light. There is a carved almsbox, signed and dated 'TB 1637'. There are some very pleasant seventeenth- and eighteenth-century houses, some of them old hunting boxes. Stocks Street, which runs through the middle of the village, housed the stocks. South of the church, the Priory, rebuilt in the nineteenth century, has a much older cottage attached to it with a west window that may be Norman.

A tunnel for the Syston-Peterborough railway was built under Manton which was the junction for Nottingham, Peterborough and Kettering.

Thomas Blore, the nineteenth-century historian of Rutland, lived in the village and was persuaded by Sir Gerald Noel to write its history which, unfortunately, was never completed.

Market Overton had a market since at least 1200, probably held on the open space just east of the church. It stands on a hill at the top of a limestone ridge and would have served as the centre for a rich agricultural region. It has long been known as

Thirteenth-century double bell-cote, St Mary's, Manton

a Roman site, later taken over by Anglo-Saxon settlers, and quantities of coins and other material have been found east of the village, just inside the borders of Thistleton parish (see Thistleton). A Roman pottery kiln has also been found to the north, in a filed called Lane Close, as well as a Saxon cemetery. One of the most interesting finds was a water clock made of very thin, perforated bronze; when put in water it took just over an hour to sink to the bottom.

It is possible that the stones used for a stile at the north end of the churchyard came from a Saxon church, though these stones, like the celebrated tower arch in the church, could be re-used Roman material.

Apart from the tower arch – important as one of the very few pieces of Roman or Saxon architecture in a Rutland church – it is worth looking at the extremely odd font made up of two capitals, the base probably Norman. The church door, as a little metal label tells us, was given to the church by William Scott, a High Sheriff of Rutland in the eighteenth century. His memorial is an unusual wall monument in the form of an open book. The sun-dial on the tower is said to have been given to the church by Isaac Newton whose grandmother lived in the village.

The church is at the west end of the village; in the centre, round the Manor House (restored in the nineteenth century), are some attractive stone houses, mostly with thatch or stone roofs. The old stocks and whipping post can be seen on the village green. To the east is a pleasant terrace of brick houses, built for the ironstone workers when the quarries reopened in 1906.

Morcott is just north of the A47, about

Norman window, St Mary the Virgin, Morcott

Normanton Tower, Rutland Water

four miles from Oakham. As you enter the village from the main road you cross the old railway line. Station Road was built in 1898 to reach the new station. It passes a Baptist chapel dating from 1732 but heavily restored in 1902.

Morcott is chiefly memorable for its beautiful Norman church, one of the most complete in the country. It has a fine Norman tower, and tower arch with carved capitals, one with entwined serpents – a symbol of eternity. Note the rare circular window in the west wall, above the fourteenth-century doorway and window, and the centre capital in the north arcade with a different carving on each face.

The Hall, now a boarding-school, is next to the Manor House (1687). The former parsonage, on the other side of the church, is dated 1627. There are many good stone houses and cottages, suggesting that there were several wealthy people in the seventeenth and eighteenth centuries. For the less fortunate Workhouse Lane (now renamed Mount Pleasant Road) led to the Uppingham Workhouse.

Morcott Windmill, now restored as a private house, stands just south of the A47, on the Barrowden road.

Normanton was one of the great estates of Rutland – the others were Exton and Burley-on-the-Hill. Now only a part of the property, the stable-block, clock tower and part of the garden, remains on shore and the church has become the best-known landmark of Rutland Water.

In the eighteenth century the estate was bought from the Mackworths by Gilbert Heathcote who was one of the founders of the Bank of England and known as 'the richest commoner in England'. A monument by Rysbrack, now in Edith Weston church, describes him as 'ready to apprehend, slow to determine, resolute to act'. Heathcote also rebuilt the sixteenth-

Buttercross, Oakham

century manor house and died in his new Hall in 1733 only eight days after he had been created a baronet. The third baronet, his grandson, pulled down the medieval church in 1764 when he enlarged his park and removed the villagers to Empingham.

The church, now shored up with concrete and reached from the shore by a causeway, is a fairly recent building. The 1826 tower and portico, which replaced the medieval bell-turret, are the work of Thomas Cundy, architect to the Grosvenor estates, who copied them from St John's Smith Square, Westminster. In 1911 the present chancel was built as a memorial to the first Earl of Ancaster. Sir Gilbert Heathcote's house was pulled down in 1925.

The church was deconsecrated when Rutland Water was created. It is now a water museum under the management of the Anglian Water Authority.

Oakham is the county town of Rutland and is most famous for its magnificent church, restored by Sir George Gilbert Scott in the nineteenth century; its Norman fortified manor house, known as Oakham Castle; and its Elizabethan grammar school, now a distinguished public school. Rutland County Museum, which is full of interesting things from Iron Age finds to agricultural machinery, is housed in the Old Riding School of the Rutland Fencibles, a force raised by the Earls of Nottingham and Gainsborough at the beginning of the nineteenth century. The District Council offices are opposite in Catmos Street.

Oakham Castle was built around 1190 by Walkelin de Ferrers, a descendant of a Norman family whose name (the same word as 'farrier') may have had something to do with the start of the custom requiring every nobleman who passed through Oak-

Inside the Castle Hall, Oakham

ham 'to do homage to the castle there in giving an horse shoe'. The earliest dated shoe belongs to the middle of the sixteenth century and some of the most recent were given by members of the present Royal Family. The whole collection is very well worth seeing. Inside, the Castle Hall is like a church, with a nave and aisles. Its arcades have beautiful, carved capitals, probably by one of the masons who worked on the chancel at Canterbury Cathedral. The west end is still arranged as a Court. Near the Castle is the church which dates from the early thirteenth century and also has some very interesting carved capitals with a variety of medieval scenes. The fourteenth-century spire and tower were probably modelled on those at Grantham. Scott's restoration (1857–9) was fairly radical and involved the rebuilding of the east end. To the north east of the church are the original buildings of Oakham School, founded by Archdeacon Johnson in 1584.

Oakham is perhaps less attractive as a town than Uppingham, partly because many of the old houses were replaced by Victorian brick buildings after the coming of the railway in 1850 brought prosperity to the town. There have also been some

unfeeling alterations, notably to the fourteenth-century Flore's House in the High Street which has suffered from a road widening. But some good buildings remain. The old Market Place has its medieval Buttercross, with the five-hole stocks still in position; near it is the only remaining Market Cross – there were once four. Other buildings worth looking at include the early eighteenth-century Judges' Lodgings (where the assize judges used to stay), some pretty red-and-blue brick houses facing each other in the High Street (the bricks made in the old Oakham brick kiln, opened in the seventeenth century) and, further west, Haynes' House, a large early eighteenth-century house. To the left a lane leads to some very good new housing on the site of old almshouses to which the Chapel of the Hospital of St John and St Anne was attached. The Chapel has been saved and restored by the District Council and was reconsecrated and opened again for services in November 1983.

Oakham has a fine modern library, built by Rutland's last county architect, Brian Kennedy. His name is commemorated in the room which houses the local history collection with many out-of-print books. Anyone at all interested in Rutland's history will want to visit it.

'Pickworth', wrote the poet John Clare, 'is a place of other days . . . it appears to be the ruins of a large town or city'. Clare worked as a lime burner at Pickworth in 1812 'and the place where we dug the kiln was full of foundations and human bones'. The foundations of the ruins then extended over two miles. In the reign of Edward III the village is said to have had taxable merchants when Oakham had none. By 1490 the village had gone – perhaps destroyed after the Battle of Empingham (1470).

Arch from old church at Pickworth

Pickworth is now a remote place, ideal for picnics or for long walks along the Drift, the old drovers' road that crosses the Great Casterton road east of the church. A fourteenth-century arch is all that remains of the medieval church. Some of the old stone must have been used for the seventeenth-century farm buildings to the north. The spire and tower survived until the eighteenth century when they were taken down to repair bridges at Wakerley and Great Casterton. The spire had become known as 'Mockbeggar' and the name appears on contemporary maps.

The 1821 church is an attempt to copy the eighteenth-century rebuilding at Tickencote nearby. It is rather charming inside with a three-decker pupit and some painted box pews.

Pilton is now a very small hamlet sandwiched between the main railway line between Peterborough and Leicester and disused railway embankments to the north (once used to transport ironstone). The quarries, which opened in 1912, have now disappeared, as have the brickworks set up to build the bridges and banks. The little church is originally thirteenth century but there were substantial restorations in the seventeenth and nineteenth centuries. The double bellcote, typical of Rutland, was probably rebuilt in the nineteenth century.

Preston is an extremely attractive ironstone village on the top of a steep hill between two valleys, about two miles south of Uppingham. The church is to the south of the main street which is full of pleasant houses, separated by grass from the road. Between the street and the main road is the seventeenth-century Manor House, across the road from the Fox and Hounds. The schoolhouse and the Hall (at the north end of Main Street) are about the same date.

The church, mostly fourteenth- and fifteenth-century on the outside, was restored in the nineteenth century when the old whitewashed plaster was, sadly, removed – the walls now look very bare. There is a richly decorated Norman arcade and a beautiful sedilia and priest's doorway (fourteenth century) in the chancel. At the entrance to the chancel are some pieces of mosaic brought from a church in Constantinople by Captain (later General) Codrington in 1925.

Ridlington is a very old village and was part of the dower of the West Saxon queens from the early tenth century. King John enclosed a royal park here from his Forest of Leighfield, and the last stag is said to have been hunted in Ridlington as late as 1800. The original church had three churches and seven hamlets dependent on it at the time of Domesday. By the middle of the nineteenth century it was little more than a ruin, with ivy hanging down inside 'in festoons' and large cracks in the walls. The whole chancel had to be taken down and was rebuilt by Halliday of Greetham: one wonders if part of the old east window

found its way to his house. Luckily he did not remove the Norman tympanum which was in two halves – one in the south chancel and the other serving as a lintel over a rather crude doorway. It represents a wheel with a lion and griffin on either side and has now been repaired. It can be seen over the vestry door.

The architect for the restoration (Henry Parsons) removed the old west gallery for the players who provided the music for the church. Their instruments have survived and can be seen in a case in the church. There is also a seventeenth-century wall monument to James Harington and his wife who lived in the manor house north of the church. The village, which had belonged to the Haringtons since 1553, has many pleasant, mostly ironstone, houses.

Ryhall has some unattractive modern houses near the Stamford-Bourne road, but don't let these put you off. This is a very pleasant, low-lying village on both sides of the River Gwash, with a pub, the Green Dragon, whose splendid thirteenth-century cellar is said to have belonged to the original Manor House. The church has even earlier associations with the seventh-century cult of St Tibba who is supposed to have had a cell here. You can see the outline of the hermitage roof on the west wall. The church is now mostly fifteenth century on the outside, though the tower and broach spire are thirteenth century. Notice the very wide nave and beautiful thirteenth-century arcades. In the chancel there is a delightful wall monument of 1696 to the son of the vicar, Samuel Barker. He was, it appears, 'a child of admirable sweetness of temper, of an erect and comely body, of a most pregnant wit, even beyond what could be imagined at the age of 2 years and 15 days'.

South of the little causeway is Foundry

Waterside, Ryhall

Road which runs beside the river and has some good stone houses. It continues to Belmesthorpe, half a mile to the south east, where there is a farm with a large stone dovecote.

Seaton, standing on high ground above the River Welland, is probably best known now for the Seaton Viaduct, built from 1876–8 to join Manton with the Kettering line to St Pancras. This monument to Victorian engineering is more than three quarters of a mile long and has eighty-four brick arches. Seaton had a period of pros-

Dovecote, Belmethorpe

Seaton Viaduct

perity while the line was being built and many temporary houses were put up. But in the depressions of the early part of this century many of the old houses fell into disrepair and have since been pulled down.

There were originally two manors in Seaton known as Up Hall and Down Hall, both of which have belonged to the Moncktons of Fineshade since the eighteenth century. Up Hall, to the east of the village near the church, is now known as the Manor House.

The twelfth-century foundations of the church (All Hallows) were discovered during the extensive restoration of 1874-5. There is a rather striking north arcade, with alternating bands of limestone and ironstone, and a beautiful chancel arch – both twelfth century. By what one historian has described as 'an act of extraordinary vandalism' the old font was chopped up and converted into a seat at the west end of the south aisle.

Thorpe-by-Water was probably a part of the manor of Down Hall and seems never to have had a church. Tudor Hall is supposed to be the old Manor House. An old road (now a footpath) crosses the present road at right angles and may have continued to Gretton.

Stoke Dry is now a hamlet of only a few houses but it is very well worth visiting both for its unusual and charming little church, on the side of a hill overlooking Eye Brook reservoir, and for the reservoir itself where you can watch birds or walk along the shore.

The church has a thin thirteenth-century tower but otherwise is mostly fifteenth century from the outside. Inside, there are many interesting things to see including the three Digby monuments (see, especially, the alabaster tomb within the altar rails, with Sir Kenelm's children on the sides of the tomb). There are also several wall paintings and two Norman columns supporting the chancel arch with very richly carved figures and foliage: there is a bell-ringer, a devil, a dragon and an eagle. One of these columns was cut away in the nineteenth century to make way for a family pew.

The Digbys owned the Manor from the fifteenth to the seventeenth centuries and one of them, Sir Everard Digby, was hanged for his part in the Gunpowder Plot. There is a local legend that the plot was hatched in the delightful little room above the church porch but as Sir Everard did not live at Stoke Dry this is unlikely. Sir Everard's son, who inherited the estate at the age of two, became a brilliant soldier, scholar and diplomat and a founder member of the Royal Society. He married a famous beauty, Venetia Stanley, who was painted by Van Dyck. Among his many publications is a fascinating cookery book, *The Closet of Sir Kenelm Digby Revealed*, which became very popular – perhaps for its thirty or so recipes for methgelin, a drink made from fermented honey. This was the drink that was traditionally served at Caldecott Feast, held each September.

Stretton, 'the town of the street', is a small village just off Ermine Street, between Tickencote and Greetham. There are some pleasant farm buildings but otherwise not a great deal to see. Edward I stopped here on his way to Scotland in 1299 and again on his way south in 1306.

The church (St Nicholas) is at the top of the village and surrounded by trees. It dates from the twelfth century but older coffin lids, one of them used as a tympanum over the south door, suggest that there must have been an earlier building here. By the late nineteenth century the church was in a terrible state. The west wall – nearly six foot thick – was leaning towards

St Andrew's, Stoke Dry

the nave; the bell turret had been injured in gales; much of the roof had gone; and the pillars of the thirteenth-century arcade were sinking into the ground. It was so carefully restored at the instigation of the Rector, Edward Bradley (a popular writer under the name of Cuthbert Bede) that it is difficult now to realize how extensive the work was.

Stocken Hall, an early seventeenth-century house just north of Stretton, is now part of a prison farm. The Ram Jam Inn, just across the A1, was a regular coaching halt called the Winchelsea Arms and is said to have got its name from the strong drink served by the landlord.

Teigh, pronounced 'tee', simply means an enclosure. It is worth visiting this very small village to see the church because it is unlike anything else you will find in Rutland. Except for the thirteenth-century

Eighteenth-century pulpit, Teigh

tower it was entirely rebuilt and re-furnished in 1782 by the Rev. Robert Sherard who was Rector for forty years and also succeeded his brother as Earl of Harborough. The architect was George Richardson and the Earl was so pleased that he used him again to build a similar church at his estate at Stapleford Park. It is only four miles away and well worth the trip.

In both churches the pews are arranged in tiers, facing the centre, as in a college choir. High up at the west end is a little pulpit, flanked by two reading-desks and overlooked by a painted landscape of trees seen through a window. Teigh has a charming mahogany font, on a brass spike, which would be brought out for christenings and placed on the altar rail. It is all delightful. The churchyard has a number of very well carved late-eighteenth-century slate gravestones. The Rectory, beside the church, was probably also built by the Earl.

Thistleton is more interesting for the past than the present. Thistles, like nettles, grow on the sites of deserted buildings and the name may date from a period after the decay of the large Roman settlement, on the borders of Thistleton and Market Overton, which was investigated in the 1950s. Maps of the site and many of the finds can be seen in the Rutland Museum though the site has been quarried away.

Thistleton is at the junction of the northern boundary of the county with Sewstern Lane, a Roman road (known also as 'the Drift) which joins Ermine Street just north of Casterton. A villa was also discovered on a site which had been occupied since the Iron Age, and a temple complex north of the Market Overton-Thistleton road.

The Manor was owned by the Brudenell family since the middle of the sixteenth century and later came into the possession of the Fludyers, who were related to the Brudenells by marriage. The medieval church was rebuilt twice; first in the 1780s by Sir George Brydges Brudenell, then an MP, and a century later – with absolutely no expense spared – by the Rector the Rev. Sir J. Henry Fludyer, Bart. The elaborate apse, a semi-octagon perhaps designed by the Rector, was his memorial to his three elder children, all of whom died of scarlet fever.

At Thistleton Gap there was a famous fight in 1811 between two boxers, Cribb and Molyneux (a Negro). Molyneux was beaten in twelve rounds and there are many prints of the occasion.

Tickencote, only half a mile from the A1, has a small church with an extraordinary and elaborately carved Norman arch. Because of this arch, which is so heavy that it has sagged in the middle, and a very early sex-partite vault, Tickencote is probably the best known of all Rutland's churches. Each of the five orders of the arch is decorated, one with the beaked heads of birds, another with many different carvings including a King's and a Queen's head looking in different directions. Over the entrance to the church is a notice informing the visitor that 'with that true sense of religion and reverence for her Maker that ever distinguished her life' Eliza Wingfield, the formidable aunt of the owner of Tickencote Hall at the time, restored the church. She was then eighty-five and died two years later, presumably highly satisfied with her architect's – S. P. Cockerell's – reconstruction of the Norman church.

'We used to go on Sundays to the Flower Pot, a little public house at Tickencoat a neighbouring village and in (one) of these excursions I first saw patty going across the fields towards her home. I was in love

Twelfth-century arch, Tickencote

at first sight . . .'. The writer was the poet John Clare and 'Sweet Patty' became his wife. The Flower Pot is no longer a pub and has lost its name; the building has been drastically restored. Down by the river is the old mill which stopped working in the 1900s.

Tinwell is close to the borders of both Lincolnshire and Northamptonshire. To the north is the A1; to the south the River Welland. It had two toll gates, one on the green beside the old smithy, the other on the Casterton road, but these have gone. The smithy, with its horseshoe in stone, is once more a forge; for many years it was the Post Office. The old village bakery, used until the 1920s, is joined to the forge.

The thirteenth-century church is unusual in having a saddleback type of roof. The Cecils of Burghley were patrons and the Manor House, directly south of the church, is said to have been a dower house for the Cecils. In the church is a Renaissance monument (1611) to the sister of the first Lord Burghley. Under the tower is a charming warning to illicit bell-ringers – perhaps seventeenth century.

Tixover church stands alone on the north shore of the River Welland, about half a mile south of the farm and the few houses that are all that is left of Tixover. The field between the farm and the church is probably the site of the old village. The base of a timber bridge and the remains of a

Horseshoe Forge, Tinwell

St Luke's, Tixover, from south

mosaic pavement have been found just south of the church, and a Roman villa to the north of Tixover Grange, on the other side of the main road.

The church, which is kept locked (key from a house near the farm), is unlike anything else you will see in Rutland and most interesting. The heavy, low unbuttressed Norman tower, seen across the fields from the Barrowden road, is one of Rutland's most attractive views; as you approach you can distinguish clearly the three beautifully simple arches of the bell-openings. Inside, there is a great tower arch, with seven roll-mouldings. This is the earliest part of the twelfth-century church, built by the French Abbey of Cluny which then owned the manor. The arcades are thirteenth century, the south being unusually earlier than the north (churches generally expanded to the north as the graveyards were on the south side). There are many other things to see, including the medieval stone seats in the chancel, some Jacobean pews, a strange corbel of a draped figure supporting the arch at the west end of the north arcade, and some interesting glass. There are some early stone coffin lids in the churchyard and a tombstone for a former rector of North Luffenham, John Weller, who chose to be buried here because he disliked his own parish – or so his own epitaph says. But maybe he also loved Tixover. Don't hurry here; it is a quiet and beautiful place to spend an afternoon.

Uppingham is a small market town, second to Oakham in size but architecturally more of a whole. The centre of the town consists of a long High Street, full of pleasant houses of all periods from the late sixteenth to the early nineteenth centuries. Several of these are shops – note, especially, the canted bay window of Baines's bakery (south-west of the crossroads), and the

Pub sign, Uppingham

Seventeenth-century house, Uppingham

59

Market Place, Uppingham

pleasant lettering on the Rutland Bookshop a few yards further west. An estate agent occupies the site of the eighteenth-century Uppingham Bookshop opposite the present shop. There has been a market in Uppingham since at least the late thirteenth century but it is now only a few stalls on a Friday. On the south side, past the Vaults, is the entrance to the church which looks north to the town and south across the churchyard to the fields. The Post Office is a very handsome eighteenth-century building on the west. Opposite, the Midland Bank (1900) has a house with decorated neo-Jacobean gables, faithfully copied after an earlier building in the same style. A fountain in the middle of the square commemorates Queen Victoria's Golden Jubilee.

Uppingham is one of the oldest of Rutland's settlements, dating from the sixth or seventh century, but it is only mentioned in the Domesday Survey as an anonymous dependency of Ridlington. The earliest remains in the church are of the early thirteenth century and these, some half figures of Christ, a saint and two angels, are now inside the church. The church was

Memorial Hall, Uppingham School

ornately restored in the nineteenth century when almost all the old fittings, including the box pews and galleries, were removed. The Elizabethan pulpit, from which the Royalist Rector of Uppingham, Jeremy Taylor, is said to have preached, is still there, however. When the Parliamentary forces approached Uppingham in 1642, Taylor, like a few other Rutland pastors, left his parish to fight for his King.

The original building of Uppingham School, founded as a Grammar School in 1584 by Archdeacon Johnson, is close to the south side of the church and has in-scriptions in Hebrew, Latin and Greek. The school grew rapidly in size and reputation during the nineteenth century, especially after the appointment in 1853 of its great headmaster, the Rev. Edward Thring. His first buildings were a chapel and science room, designed by the well-known Victorian architect, G. E. Street. Later buildings are by St Thomas Jackson, a distinguished architect who came originally from Stamford, and Sir Ernest Newton, an Old Uppinghamian who designed the Memorial Hall, with ideas taken from Kirby Hall, and the War Memorial Chapel.

Uppingham is a good place for pubs, probably because it has had a market for so long. Facing the Market Place is the Falcon and, near it, the old sign of the Unicorn (no longer a pub). Both buildings date from the seventeenth century. Then there are the Vaults in the Market Place (the old Duke of Wellington), the White Hart opposite the School, the Exeter Arms further west, and several others.

Wardley lies on the south-west border of Rutland and its name suggests a look-out ('weard') in a clearing ('leah'). It has now only a few houses straggling down a steep hill to the south of the Uppingham-Leicester road. The village must once have been larger; the church dates from the twelfth century (south door) and one can see the lines of the roof of the first church on the east of the tower. The chancel was entirely rebuilt in 1871 but the old box pews remained, although their doors have gone. There is an eighteenth-century font, some Commandment Boards and a delightful small barrel organ.

Whissendine is a large, scattered village, divided by the Whissendine Brook. Many of its inhabitants live in the new estates, built in the last ten years or so for commuters to Leicester and Nottingham. But there was also quite a lot of building in the nineteenth century and the stone foundations of several low old cottages can be found below the newer brick. The oldest part of the village is to the east where the magnificent church of St Andrew stands on a small hill, facing south. It is one of Rutland's largest and most imposing churches and its plan is similar to those of Langham and Oakham. The best view of the Perpendicular tower is from the north; on the south and west the harmony of the bell tower is spoiled by the decision (of the original designer) to put in a staircase

(Pevsner). Inside, much of the church is thirteenth century. There is a lovely fifteenth-century clerestory and oak roof which has carved wall posts of hooded figures, some of them playing musical instruments. When Sir George Gilbert Scott restored the church in 1865 it was hoped that money would be found to re-build the window in the south transept of the chancel whose top had been cut off at some time, perhaps in the seventeenth century. However, the money was not forthcoming. Whissendine acquired a beautiful screen from St John's College, Cambridge, when Scott rebuilt the chapel there.

To the east of the church is the Manor House, built by the Sherard family in the seventeenth century. It is now a farmhouse.

Whitwell village now has only a cluster of cottages and a farm (on the site of the Old Hall) at the edge of Rutland Water. There is also a pub, the Noel Arms, much used by the fishermen from the Fishing Lodge which is at the end of the road to the reservoir. For about three centuries the manor belonged to the Prior of St John of Jerusalem but it was confiscated by Henry VIII in 1540 and about a century later came into the possession of the Noels of Exton who, until the 1950s, owned much of the village.

The village seems to get its name from a well west of the church which occasionally flooded into the building through two holes which can be seen at the foot of the most eastern pillar in the nave arcade. Unfortunately St Michael's was filled with rather bad stained glass in the nineteenth century, making the interior very dark.

Within the altar rails, on the north side, is a recess which could have been an old altar bread oven. The church has no fewer than four piscinas, each indicating

1830s drawing showing Wing church with spire

that there was an altar here in the middle ages. One altar has been re-used as a grave stone. The American organ comes from Normanton church.

There were some very interesting excavations here during 1976–7 (details at the Rutland Museum). An Iron Age enclosure was found and subsequently a Roman-British farmstead and other buildings on the same site.

Wing is about three miles south of Uppingham, on a hill above the Chater valley. The view east to the church down the main street has not changed a great deal in the last hundred years though the buildings of the Cuckoo Inn (near the church) and the King's Arms (further east) have been extended. There are still many good stone houses of the sixteenth to eighteenth centuries and Wing is a pleasant village to walk round.

The church, St Peter and St Paul, lost its spire in 1841/2, probably because the new Rector, Charles Boys, was worried that the spire might fall or damage the Rectory which he was repairing. It had not been lived in for at least twelve years and stood right up against the west wall of the church. There has been a lot of restoration and from the outside the church is largely nineteenth century – the chancel was completely rebuilt in 1875. But inside the modern porch is a late Norman doorway; there is also a mid-twelfth-century arcade of three bays. When the tower was built in the late fourteenth century the western bay of the nave was shortened and half an arcade on each side was cut away.

Near the church is an old turf maze, perhaps dating from the middle ages. It is about forty feet in diameter and may have been used for doing penance; wrongdoers would crawl round the maze on their hands and knees. There is a similar maze at Alkborough in North Lincolnshire.

In the nineteenth century Wing had a Wise Woman called Amelia Woodcock. She was a healer who was widely known for her herbal remedies. She died in 1867.

Stockerston Hill, looking toward Belton